IRAN

The ruins of old mosques are found throughout Iran;
this one makes an imaginative playground for children
living in the hilly region near Zenjan.

THIS BEAUTIFUL WORLD   VOL. 45

IRAN

BANRI NAMIKAWA

KODANSHA INTERNATIONAL LTD.
TOKYO, NEW YORK & SAN FRANCISCO

Distributors:
UNITED STATES: *Harper & Row, Publishers, Inc., 10 East 53rd Street, New York, New York 10022.* CANADA: *Fitzhenry & Whiteside Limited, 150 Lesmill Road, Don Mills, Ontario.* CENTRAL AND SOUTH AMERICA: *Feffer & Simons Inc., 31 Union Square, New York, New York 10003.* BRITISH COMMONWEALTH (*excluding Canada and the Far East*): *TABS, 51 Weymouth Street, London W1.* EUROPE: *Boxerbooks Inc., Limmatstrasse 111, 8031 Zurich.* AUSTRALIA AND NEW ZEALAND: *Paul Flesch & Co. Ltd., 259 Collins Street, Melbourne 3000.* THAILAND: *Central Department Store Ltd., 306 Silom Road, Bangkok.* HONG KONG: *Books for Asia Ltd., 379 Prince Edward Road, Kowloon.* THE FAR EAST: *Japan Publications Trading Company, P.O. Box 5030, Tokyo International, Tokyo.*

Published by Kodansha International Ltd., 2-12-21 Otowa, Bunkyo-ku, Tokyo 112 and Kodansha International/USA, Ltd., 10 East 53rd Street, New York, New York 10022 and 44 Montgomery Street, San Francisco, California 94104. Copyright © 1973 by Kodansha International Ltd. All rights reserved. Printed in Japan.

LCC 73-79762
ISBN 0-87011-213-9
JBC 0326-784142-2361

First edition, 1973

Contents

ACKNOWLEDGMENTS

I wish to express my gratitude to the following people for their cooperation in making this book possible.

H. E. Astollah Alam, Minister of Court

H. E. Hamid Rahnema, Minister of Information

H. E. Abbas Ali Khalatbari, Minister of Foreign Affairs

H. E. Kambiz Yazdan-Panah, Ministry of Court

H. E. Farhad Nikoukhah, Deputy Minister of Information

H. E. M. A. Samii, Deputy Minister of Information

H. E. Abdol Hossein Hamzavi, Iranian Ambassador to Japan

Mr. F. Nouredin Kia, Ministry of Foreign Affairs

Mr. Mahmud Salehi, Ministry of Foreign Affairs

Mr. Cyrus Farahmandi, Ministry of Information

Mr. Hadi Sharifian, Ministry of Information

Mr. Iradge Pezeshgzad, Ministry of Foreign Affairs

Dr. A. Shahidzadeh, Director, Tehran Archaeological Museum

Dr. M. H. Semsar, Director, Tehran Decorative Museum

H. E. Kensaku Maeda, Japanese Ambassador to Iran

Mr. Eiji Inoue, Embassy of Japan, Tehran

The Dream of Shah Abbas

ISFAHAN is half the world. So went the saying after the provincial town of Isfahan had, almost overnight, become one of the handsomest cities of the sixteenth century and the capital of one of the century's most remarkable monarchs, Shah Abbas the Great. Although he had formidable competition among his contemporaries—Queen Elizabeth I of England, Emperor Charles V of Spain, and Sultan Suleiman of Turkey—Shah Abbas manifestly holds his own as warrior, diplomat, administrator, builder, patron of the arts and sciences, and ruler of wisdom and tolerance.

But Shah Abbas comes late in Isfahan's history, and to call it a provincial town before he made it his capital is perhaps to do it something of an injustice, since owing to its strategic geographical position it was a place of importance as far back as the third millennium B.C. That was the time when Iranians separated into two distinct groups, one heading toward the west into Media, the other to the south into what the outside world for many centuries called Persia (from Parsa or Fars, the name of the southwestern part of Iran). The Iranians themselves, however, called the region Aryana, "land of the Aryans," or in middle Persian, Eran, and now officially Iran.

The first known establishment of any importance of these southern Iranians was Isfahan. Indeed, it was here that the celebrated founder of the Persian nation is said to have built a fortress that was still standing in the tenth century A.D. In between those two dates, Isfahan saw the rise and fall of many dynasties —Achaemenian, Alexandrian, Seleucid, Parthian, Sassanian— although it did not itself play a leading role comparable to that of Persepolis to the south.

The conquering Arabs first entered Iran in the seventh century, when they founded four caliphates there. These, in the course of time, were torn by sectarian strife, for Iran, with its long history of absolutism and monarchy, tended to adhere to the Shi'ite sect of Islam, which believed the supreme caliphate to be hereditary and divine, descending only from Ali, nephew of Mohammed and fourth caliph. The more widespread Sunnite party, on the other hand, held that the caliphate was an elective office to be filled only by members of the Quraysh tribe of Mecca.

It was this division of belief and consequent dynastic squabbles that facilitated the Mongol conquest of Iran, during which Timur (or Tamerlane, as he is also called) surrounded Isfahan and at the gate of the city constructed a tower of seventy thousand skulls as an indication of what might happen to those who rebelled. The Mongol reign was ultimately put down at the beginning of the sixteenth century by Ismail, who assumed the title of shah and founded the ardently pro-Shi'ite dynasty of the Safawids, named after his ancestor Safi ud-Din.

His reign, as well as that of his successors, was plagued by constant struggle with the Ottoman sultans, who were Sunnite by faith and conquerors by inclination. When Abbas eventually ascended the throne in 1587 at the age of sixteen, his country was hopelessly divided and impoverished, ruled largely by tribal chieftains. But Abbas, a true military genius, first made peace with the Turks, who occupied part of the country, then subdued the rival chiefs, defeated the advancing Uzbeks, and finally drove the Turks out of Persia. In this latter feat he was assisted by a group of Europeans under the leadership of Sir Anthony Sherley, who had been sent by the Earl of Essex to help this self-proclaimed enemy of the Turks and also to try to improve trade relations between England and Persia. By the beginning of the seventeenth century Shah Abbas was ruler of a reunited country.

Now he was able to turn a greater share of both his time and wealth to the arts of peace, to the rebuilding of his country, and in particular to the glorification of his new capital, Isfahan. Realizing the importance of foreign trade, he built factories to cater to merchants from all over Europe, and, although a devout Moslem, was pleased to receive ambassadors from the Christian states. To beautify his capital and to attract visitors to it, he erected palaces and mosques, markets and schools, baths and caravansaries, and spacious bridges across the city's river. A Frenchman who lived in Isfahan at the end of the century estimated its population to be in the neighborhood of six hundred thousand, a tremendous figure in those days.

Abbas's record, unfortunately, is not unblemished. Like many other rulers of his time, he attempted to ensure his longevity somewhat ruthlessly: he had his eldest son killed and another blinded. After his death, his great and beautiful city gradually declined. At the beginning of the eighteenth century came the Afghan invasion; a few years later, Karim Khan transferred his seat of government to Shiraz, and by the end of the century Tehran had been captured by Agha Mohammed Khan, a eunuch chieftain, who made it his capital.

During this time a number of Isfahan's buildings simply vanished, while in the first years of the present century a government commission decided to repair only a few of the remaining constructions and to raze the others. So tremendous, however, had been Shah Abbas's building fervor and so superb his taste that some of the handsomest buildings in the whole Islamic world are still to be found in Isfahan. Among them is one that critics consider to be the finest of all, as well as one of the most beautiful buildings in the world, the Masjid-i-Shah, the Mosque of the Shah, or, as it is more commonly called, the Royal Mosque.

I think it is virtually impossible to describe an edifice as justly famous as this. An architect will certainly want to study its plan, its building methods, the construction of its arches and great dome, and the different kinds of marble and tile used. He may well find it incomparably superior to the celebrated mosques of Istanbul. A historian will probably want to know the date the mosque was built, how many years were involved in the process, and why Shah Abbas, who had already erected several mosques in Isfahan, undertook in 1612 the construction of this, the largest and most magnificent of them all. The tourist will marvel at the five hundred different kinds of tiles used in its decoration. The devout pilgrim will stand in reverence before the familiar Islamic creed: "There is no God but God, and Mohammed is his Prophet. God is great."

But everyone, I think, pilgrim or tourist, architect or historian, will wander through the vast structure completely hypnotized by its subtle and seductive lines, its halls and chambers, courtyard and central shrine all tiled in a variety of delicate colors, and he will think that he has walked into a wonderland, a world of the gods beyond the powers of man to create. He will thank divine providence for bringing him into this miraculous edifice. He will, as I did, depart in silence, and later in the silence of his mind he will reevoke that mystical experience, knowing that only a poet or a genius could find words to do it justice; and if he is wise, he will refrain from trying.

Inevitably I began to wonder about the importance of mosques to the Islamic people, particularly because in Japan, a temperate country, although we subscribe to both Buddhism and Shintoism, we acknowledge no supreme and absolute deity. I know that comparative religion is a highly specialized study, and it is unfair to make rash generalizations, but from my travels around the world, I have made one observation. It seems to me that the places where Islam, in its purest form, has taken strongest hold over the people are the hot countries, and very often countries that have large areas of desert.

In contrast to the arid, yellow, monotonous desert, the mosque is dark, cool, and restful. It is decorated in soothing blues and greens, its marble floors are cool to the unshod foot, and the chanting of the Koran is hypnotic, impersonal, and reassuring, unlike the harsh struggle for existence outside its walls. And above all, the cool, dark, yet zealous atmosphere of the mosque creates an irresistible appeal, where the worshipper feels immediately he is in direct communion with a supreme deity who promises solace in the next world in return for hardships endured in this one.

And that, I think, is one of the reasons, Islam maintains so strong a hold on its people. It began in the desert, where life is bitter, and it persists in those countries where life continues to be a daily struggle. In the desert man must fight for his livelihood; he stands alone to face the sun, the moon, the stars, the rolling sand dunes, and nothing else. He seeks the solace of the supernatural, and he willingly accepts the absolutism of Islam. Although the religion of Mohammed grew out of the other two great monotheistic religions, Judaism and Christianity, it is more rigid and authoritarian than either. Once it had been enunciated by the Prophet, Islam spread like wildfire, not only because powerful Arabian armies carried it with them but also because the countries it was brought to were on the whole poor countries whose people desperately needed the certainty of a reward after death. I think I am safe in saying that of all the nations where Islam has been introduced, only Spain eventually rejected it.

Iran is devoutly Islamic, and as I have said earlier, mainly Shi'ite, and as in other Islamic countries, one frequently hears expressions of total submission to God, to Allah, for that is what the word *Islam* means: "resignation, surrender." It is so closely woven into the language that people in the countryside will not speak without immediately adding, "if God wills." If a farmer's tractor breaks down, he will say, as people do in the Islamic world, "It is written." But are there no parts available to repair the tractor in the village? That too its written. Does the bus taking him to the nearest town to purchase the needed parts break down? It is written. Do the parts he buys not fit the tractor after all? It is written. There is nothing to be done but resign oneself to the inevitable.

Many observers feel that the sense of stagnation that permeates the present-day Islamic world is due to this fatalistic view of life. Here, no doubt, I shall be getting into hot water, for I feel that that particular kind of fatalism did not characterize the religion of Mohammed when it was at its height. Islam today has lost its original dynamism, and the fact that in the Islamic countries religion has never been divorced from government impedes those countries from keeping up with the rest of the world. In its orthodoxy, the Islamic faith has condemned new inventions, and so it is responsible to a certain degree for the backwardness of its people. If the predominantly Christian countries of the West may speak of the tragedy of man who has lost God, then perhaps the Islamic countries should question the tragedy of man who has not lost God, the man who has shifted the burdens that he should bear himself onto the shoulders of God.

There may have been something of this feeling in the shahanshah of Iran, himself a devout Moslem, when he proclaimed his "Revolution of the Shah and the People" (which came to be called the "white revolution") in 1963, but more about that later on. Right now I think it is time to return once more to Isfahan, the old Islamic capital and the living proof that the one quality Shah Abbas and his people did not possess was passivity. It has been estimated that Isfahan at its height boasted over one hundred and fifty mosques, nearly two thousand caravansaries, some fifty schools, and close to three hundred public baths. Its population, as I noted earlier, was around six hundred thousand, somewhat more than it is today. Around the walls of the city were clustered fifteen hundred small villages, including one for Christian Armenians, who built their own churches, and one for Jews, who were also permitted to observe their own religious rites.

Today the chief remaining sights of the old capital (except for the very large and ancient, splendidly domed Masjid-i-Jami) center around the Meidan-i-Shah, the Persian word *meidan* meaning a broad open area, such as a parade ground or esplanade. Here, in addition to the Royal Mosque, stands the small but lovely Masjid-i-Sheik Luftullah, which Shah Abbas consecrated to the memory of his uncle, a man famed for his piety, and which the shah used for his private devotions. Here also is the Ali Kapu, an impressive, ancient palace with a huge veranda, from which the royal court observed the activities in the square below. The Ali Kapu overlooks the extensive Royal Gardens, where the Chihil Situn is situated, a throne room used chiefly for the reception of distinguished visitors and ambassadors.

At the north end of the Meidan-i-Shah rises a monumental gateway that leads to the royal bazaar, the Kaisarieh. Here, in an enormous area, the visitor may stroll for some three miles under the shade of awnings and porticoes, marveling at the famous arts and crafts of Iran, of which Isfahan is still the chief producer. Metalwork, mosaic inlay, carpets, brocades, hand-blocked printed cloth—the wide-eyed visitor may pay his money and take his choice. Although many of these crafts are very ancient in Iranian history, they, like so much else, were revived during the golden age of the seventeenth century. Moslem taboos on representations of human or animal forms are no longer strictly observed in these decorative arts.

Naturally enough, the Abbasid renaissance also affected the fine arts of Persia, such as painting and calligraphy, book production and illustration, music and literature, as well as history and poetry. Of course, the most famous of Persian poetry and miniatures antedate Shah Abbas, but the ferment of his new capital gave rise to a wealth of book-making and to a famous school of painting. The deeds of the shah himself were chronicled in a well-known history written by Iskandar-munshi.

The language spoken in Iran today, by the way, is very similar to that used in the Abbasid capital. It is clearly descended from the ancient tongue, used as early as the third century A.D., called Middle Persian, although the modern language has borrowed, along with its alphabet, a number of characteristics of Arabic.

A few years ago, the Linguistics Section of the Congress of Iranologists met in Tehran and recommended the adoption of a new system of transliteration of Persian into Roman script. But those recommendations have not been generally followed outside of Iran, and the older, no doubt inaccurate, forms remain more familiar. The Iranologists, for instance, in writing about Isfahan (Esfahān), speak of the Masjed-e-Sāh and the Qeysariyyeh as having been built by Sāh Abbās; but this seems to me to make an already difficult language still more difficult for the reader, and so at the risk of incurring the wrath of Tehran I have preferred to use the familiar forms. I hope the Iranologists will forgive me, and I hope the great Sāh Abbās, to whom I feel deeply indebted for a rich and unique experience, will forgive me too.

1-2. The two deserts of Iran, Dasht-e Kavir and Dasht-e Lut (*preceding pages*), account for one sixth of the country's total area and are the most arid in the world.

3-5. Isfahan (*right*), the capital built by Shah Abbas the Great in 1598 centers around a huge square, the Meidan-i-Shah (*below*), on the south side of which lies the city's most magnificent building, the Royal Mosque (*opposite*).

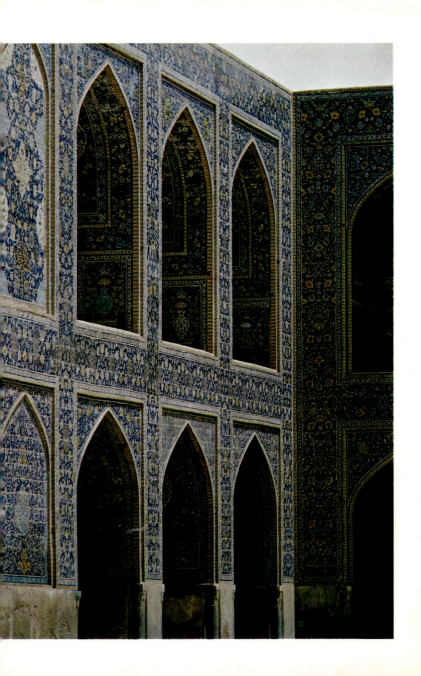

6-8. Inside the Royal Mosque: the great dome of the
main prayer hall (*above*), decorated archways (*opposite*),
and the central courtyard (*overleaf*).

9-10. The Ali Kapu Palace (*below*) on the
western side of the Meidan-i-Shah, used to be a
royal residence with a large veranda, from
which the court watched ceremonies held in the
square below; *opposite*, a decorative detail from
the lavish interior.

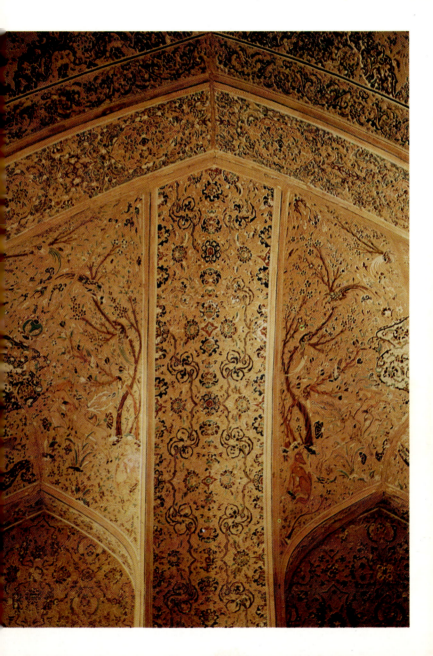

11-14. Isfahan is well known for textiles, carpets, metalwork and traditional Iranian handicrafts; *right*, a fruit vendor; *below*, a narrow alley and a shop in the Meidan-i-Shah; *opposite*, a stall in Isfahan's royal bazaar, the Kaisarieh.

15-16. After a carpet is woven it is first washed under running water (*below*), then hung over a wall to dry under the watchful eyes of one of the women (*opposite*).

17. A narrow lane in the old quarter of Isfahan provides respite from the hot sun.

Commemoration of Empire

I considered myself most fortunate to have been invited to attend, along with five Japanese archaeologists, the once-in-a-lifetime festivities marking the 2500th anniversary of the founding of the Persian Empire by Cyrus the Great. At this glamorous event, which took place in October, 1971, our hosts were His Imperial Majesty Mohammed Reza Pahlavi, Shahanshah Aryamehr, and his wife, Empress Farah; the guests of honor were over fifty heads of state or their representatives, including kings and queens, presidents and prime ministers, princes and princesses.

"We do not consider this anniversary to be a purely national event," said our host, "but rather one that belongs to the whole human community." The shah's words can hardly be quarreled with, for if Iran was not the sole cradle of human civilization, it was one of the few very important ones. Cyrus, a man of action and compassion, began life as the son of the leader of the Achaemenian clan, one of the Pasargadae tribes, and before his death, had become, in the words of the prophet Ezra, "king of the world, great king, mighty king, king of Babylon, king of the land of Sumer and Akkad, king of the four quarters."

The story of how he accomplished this extraordinary task has, of course, been overlaid with legend, but there is no question that he did become ruler of the mightiest empire the world had then known. Nor is there any question either that, far from turning into a tyrant, he remained a capable as well as a humane administrator. Those whom he conquered were treated with a kindliness unequaled in the ancient world. A notable example is Babylonia, where he ruled, in the words of one historian, like "a constitutional monarch." The Jews captive in Babylonia he permitted to return to Jerusalem and rebuild their temple, which may be why he is referred to in the Book of Isaiah as the anointed of the Lord.

Cyrus's favorite capital was Pasagardae, which he built and named after his own tribe, and here, upon his death around the year 529 B.C., he was buried in a very simple tomb, unlike the huge and ornate mausoleums of so many monarchs of the ancient Middle East. Cyrus's tomb is still to be seen, but his body and the treasures that almost certainly accompanied it have disappeared without trace. His greatest monument is still his country, where he is regarded as the father of his people, and it was in his country that the present ruler set out to do him honor with the anniversary festivities.

The most impressive event of the elaborate program was the grand two-hour procession that took place on October 15 at Persepolis, the once splendid capital founded by Darius the Great in 515 B.C., then taken and destroyed some two centuries later by Alexander the Great. Between those two events, successive monarchs constructed one of the handsomest cities of the ancient world, a fact to which the impressive ruins testify most eloquently. The Persian name of the city is Takht-e-Jamshid, "Throne of Jamshid," a mythical Iranian king with whom the foundation of the city is legendarily associated. The Greek name, Persepolis, is a grim play on words, for it may mean either "City of Persia" (*Pérsai*) or "City of Destruction" (*Pérsis*).

The grand afternoon procession was not only exciting and colorful but was also a careful and scholarly reevocation of the various dynasties that have ruled Iran. Thus spectators were able to enjoy in highly dramatic form a capsule history of the country, from a prehistoric standard-bearer to corpsmen and corpswomen of the shahanshah's white revolution.

The founding dynasty, the Achaemenian, was represented by brilliantly clad standard-bearers, officers and soldiers of both infantry and cavalry, and horse-drawn chariots of different types. For each participant in the parade, the official program gave a list of sources that were consulted to ensure accuracy. The program also listed the dynasty's major accomplishments, beginning with the uniting of the Aryan people and the imperial foundation of Iran, and ending with the world's first attempt to build a canal linking the Red Sea and the Mediterranean.

The rulers of the Achaemenian dynasty, embroiled in one way or another in internal Greek strife, undertook missions of subjugation and conquest, most of which ended in defeat. Further weakened by the corruption that all too frequently accompanies absolute power, the dynasty was overthrown by Alexander the Great. Before Alexander's death in Babylon in 323 B.C., some ten thousand of his officers and men were married, in a mass wedding feast at Susa, to Persian wives.

Then, for nearly a century after his death, Persia was racked by Greek dynastic squabbles, which ended only with the rise of the Arsacids, who founded the Parthian empire. This, destined to endure until the third century A.D., was the second dynasty represented in the Persepolis parade. Here there were a number of cavalry officers and soldiers, men and mounts alike heavily armored, suggestive of the belligerent Parthians, who were constantly at war with Rome. Rather halfheartedly attempting to carry on the traditions of the Achaemenian dynasty, they publicly acknowledged Zoroastrian doctrine, raising altars to the holy power of fire, and called themselves king of kings, which is the meaning of shahanshah, the title of Iran's present monarch.

With the dynasty that followed, the Sassanian, fire worship was once again strongly reaffirmed, for the founder of that dynasty was a native of Pérsis, where the cult of Zoroaster had been zealously followed for centuries. He is known to the Iranians as Ardashir, although he also called himself Artaxerxes, after his Achaemenian predecessors. The dynasty he founded, which lasted for more than four centuries and included nearly thirty kings of kings, was periodically at war with the Romans, then with the emerging Turks, and finally with the Arabs, who accomplished its downfall.

By the middle of the seventh century, Moslem Arabs had occupied almost all of Iran, which was partitioned into four caliphates and which soon fell altogether under the spell of the Koran. Although Arab rulers, generally speaking, tolerated Zoroastrianism, the ancient fire religion could not withstand the assaults of the more powerful monotheism of Mohammed. There is still a small group of believers in the country today, while outside Iran the chief practitioners of Zoroastrianism are the Parsees of Bombay.

The centuries that followed were marked by sectarian strife within the country as well as by incursions from abroad by the Seljuks and the Mongols. The two dynasties of this period represented in the Persepolis procession were the Saffarid (867–908) and the Dailamite (932–1062). It was during this time that Herat, in present-day Afghanistan, became a flourishing center of Persian culture under the Timurid monarchs, Shahrukh and his son Ulugh Beg, the famous astronomer.

Finally in 1502 came Ismail, the first of the Safawid shahs, and then towards the end of the century Abbas the Great, under whose rule the country was unified and revitalized and the Shi'ite branch of Islam established as the national religion. In the procession, we saw warriors wearing the colorful uniforms that have been made so familiar to us through Persian miniatures and drawings. Here in the amber ruins of Persepolis, Shah Abbas's glowing capital seemed further away than a couple of hundred miles, or even a couple of thousand years.

After his death, as we have seen, the dynasty fell into gradual decline, leaving Iran open to adventurism by the Afghans, followed by the Russians and the Turks. At length there rose the Afshar tribesman, Nadr Kuli Beg, son of an impoverished family in the Province of Khurasan, who was destined to become one of Iran's greatest generals. He drove the foreign invaders from his homeland and eventually found himself ruler of his country. At that time he took the name of Nadir Shah, by which he is known today.

During the first years of his quarter-century reign, Nadir Shah continued to demonstrate his military genius. By 1739, he occupied both Kandahar and Delhi, the latter for a period of two months, from where he removed incalculable treasure: "the accumulated wealth," in the words of an Indian historian, "of three hundred and forty-eight years." This included the Peacock Throne, estimated to be worth over thirty million dollars. Unfortunately, success spoiled Nadir Shah, as it has spoiled most military men who have risen to supreme power. He blinded his eldest son, whom he unfairly accused of plotting against him, and put so many of his officers to death that he was finally assassinated by his own bodyguard. His country, which had every reason to be grateful to him, could only breathe a sigh of relief at news of his death. His warriors in the Persepolis procession were shown mounted not only on horses but also on the camels that he used to such stunning effect in some of his campaigns.

Following this came the soldiers of the Zand rulers and then of the Qajars, kings who presided over two unhappy and troubled centuries in Iranian history. It was a time of poverty and uncertainty, of struggle among the power hungry elite and threats from foreign governments with colonial ambitions, a time that happily came to a close in 1925 with the election by a constituent assembly of Riza Khan, the minister of war, to the monarchy.

A most capable ruler, Riza Shah Pahlavi inaugurated the reforms that his eldest son, who ascended the throne in 1941, has carried forward with such conspicuous success. At his coronation, the present shahanshah announced that he would rule as a constitutional monarch, and some ten years ago inaugurated his so-called white revolution, which has indeed been both white, or bloodless, and revolutionary. The grand procession that began with a prehistoric standard-bearer came to a stirring end with a troop of young men and women dedicated to furthering that bloodless revolution.

As I drove along the forty-mile road from the ruins of Persepolis to the city of Shiraz—a road lined for the occasion, appropriately and dramatically, with flickering Zoroastrian fires set at fifty-yard intervals—I could not help wondering how successful the shahanshah and his dedicated youth are destined to be in their struggle to modernize and, in the deepest sense, to remake their country.

True, they have so far accomplished a tremendous, almost unbelievable, lot in developing the economy of the country, in taking over the management of the all-important oil production, in reforming a feudal land tenure system, in eradicating illiteracy, in raising the nation's overall standard of living. Yet the greatest problem, it seems to me, still remains to be solved: the problem of water. Some 70 percent of the country's surface is either desert or bare mountain, and unless Iran succeeds in redeeming a substantial portion of that waste land by bringing water to it, will the country ever know true prosperity and security?

A second very serious problem, from my point of view, is the state religion. Islam, as I noted earlier, in its orthodoxy and rigidity, tends to reject what it is not already familiar with. Indeed, some of its most zealous practitioners would like to reject everything that Mohammed himself was not familiar with —hardly an encouraging attitude for a people who must make the giant leaps that the twentieth century's technological era demands. Religion, we have been told by the so-called communists, is the opiate of the people. While I certainly do not subscribe to that dictum, I find that in Islamic countries it may easily become a deterrent to progress. With nothing but admiration for the accomplishments of the white revolution, I could not help entertaining doubts about its ultimate success until, or unless, it manages to resolve these two problems.

The following summer I was back in Shiraz to meet my associates, with whom I was to travel and take pictures. This was their first visit to Iran, and as they got off the plane at Shiraz they were full of wonder at the bleak, imposing mountains they had glimpsed from the air, bordering an equally bleak salt desert, stretching off toward the east as far as they could see. I pointed out to them that those two great deserts of the central plateau, the Lut and the Kavir, occupy a full sixth of the six hundred thousand square miles that constitute Iran's total land area. I had two more dry statistics to give them: of the country's estimated twenty-six million people, over 60 percent live in rural areas, yet less than 10 percent of the land is arable.

We drove into Shiraz, where once again there was general astonishment, this time at its many green trees and perfumed gardens. Shiraz is above all a Mohammedan city, located, according to the poet Hafiz, in "an incomparable situation." Lying

some five thousand feet above sea level, it borders a well-watered plain, which enabled its Mohammedan rulers to indulge, to the fullest extent, their passion for gardens. Some of these have fallen into neglect, but enough remain to make it an extraordinarily pleasant city to visit and wander through.

Although its original foundation dates back to the Achaemenian dynasty, there are few very ancient remains. Even its well-stocked museum possesses little that antedates the arrival of the Arabs, and its chief monuments are its mosques, schools and, of course, its gardens. Even though it was for a brief time the capital of the country, and though many of Iran's monarchs, including the great Shah Abbas, initiated building projects, it never equaled Isfahan in this respect, nor have earthquakes, which hit the city several times, been kind to it.

Its most conspicuous claim to fame is its two illustrious poets, Saadi and Hafiz, who take unquestioned place in the first rank of Persia's poets. Both are enshrined in handsome modern mausoleums in their native city. "O God!" cried Hafiz in an ode to Shiraz, "Preserve it from decline!" Although God has not altogether obliged, since Shiraz has declined somewhat from its greatest days, it remains one of the country's most important and beautiful cities, a major agricultural and handicraft center, and a stepping-off place for the nation's chief ancient monument, Persepolis.

Some of the better preserved monuments of ancient Egypt and the Middle East, of Greece and Rome are perhaps more famous, but none are as moving, or as vital to Western history and culture, as Persepolis. A guide to the ruins published by the Ministry of Information on the occasion of the anniversary celebrations quotes J. H. Iliffe, director of the City of Liverpool Museums, who wrote in his book *Legacy of Persia*: "Considering the tremendous role which Aryan man has played in world history, how unfamiliar to us (his Western descendants) are his origins and the lands that were the cradle of his race. Hebrew, Greek and Roman civilization is absorbed, more or less, by Western man with his mother's milk; the vast Iranian panorama in which his ancestors arose and flourished seems as remote to the majority as the moon." Thanks to the shahanshah's determination to celebrate that 2500th anniversary as splendidly as possible, the cradle of the Aryan race no longer seems as remote as the moon. (Of course it may also be argued that the moon no longer seems very remote either.)

One of the reasons cited by historians for the importance of Persepolis to Western civilization is its possession of a comprehensive library, which Alexander had translated into Greek before destroying it. Thus Persepolis, by way of Greece, exerted a profound influence on all human culture, and one of the ironies of history is that the vast and world-famous library in the Egyptian city that Alexander founded, which still bears his name, was ultimately destroyed by Arab conquerors. As one scans the story of man, from Persepolis to Nazi book burnings and Soviet censorship, one wonders how human civilization has managed to survive at all, for there appears to be a profound antipathy between tyrants (even one so enlightened as Alexander) and ideas; and when the human race has to choose between them, it still seems to prefer the former.

Such were our rather gloomy conclusions as we wandered those hot summer days in and around Persepolis, trying to flesh out the bare bones that remain. It was Darius I who, after subduing minor uprisings, conceived the stupendous project of building a capital city worthy of the newly regained position of the Achaemenians as great kings, mighty kings, kings of the four quarters, kings of the world, kings of kings. Clearly, to justify titles so resounding, a king must possess a worthy palace, and there was nothing petty about Darius's architectural visions.

Choosing a strategic location at the foot of the high rocky hill once called the Royal Mountain and now known as the Mount of Mercy, he began the construction of a tremendous terrace with a total area of over one hundred and fifty thousand square yards. Atop this terrace he and his son Xerxes built the Apadana, the "kingliest palace," consisting of a huge audience hall (over four thousand square yards in area) flanked by porches, with service rooms at each of its four corners, antechambers that connected the audience hall with the great king's private palace and lesser private palaces.

Of course it is quite impossible for us today to imagine the splendor of the Apadana after it was finally completed and before it was put to pillage and the torch, for the great kings had virtually the entire known world to draw upon. They brought vermilion crystal from Sogdiana and blue crystal from Chorasmia and gold in unimaginable quantities, for gold was then, as it is now, the most coveted of metals. The great doors were covered with gold, decorations were of gold, statues were embellished with gold, the royal bodyguard wore accoutrements of gold, heavy curtains were made of gold lace, and of course the throne was of gold. It was a hall intended to overawe the vassal kings who came bringing tribute to the king of kings, amid the sound of music and the smoke of incense curling upward from gold and silver bowls. We decided there could be little question that the hall must have more than fulfilled its builders' aim.

Of all the bare bones still standing in Persepolis, perhaps the most impressive is the elaborately sculptured grand staircase of the Apadana. Here, in three distinct rows, we see tribute being brought to the king of kings by conquered peoples: Medes, Elamites, Parthians, Sogdians, Egyptians, and Bactrians; Armenians, Babylonians, Scythians, Assyrians, and Thracians; Phoenicians, Cappadocians, Lydians, Aracosians, and Indians. Among the tribute were decorative objects, articles of clothing, weapons of all sorts, domesticated animals, and vessels filled with gold. I tried to picture that colorful procession but my prosaic twentieth-century imagination was quite unequal to the task.

Late one afternoon, we climbed the steep slope of the Mount of Mercy, passing the tombs of three of the Achaemenian kings and the site of the channel that was dug to bring water from the hills to the city, until we reached a vantage point from which we could see Persepolis lying before us in all its ruined grandeur. As the sun lowered, we picked out the monuments over which we had wandered: the grand staircase leading to the terrace, the Porch of Xerxes at the top, with its colossal bas-reliefs of winged bulls, the carvings and columns of the palaces, and the remains of the treasury.

Here again, imagination fails. The guidebook tells us that the treasures of Persepolis were worth some twelve hundred million gold francs, but it does not tell us when that estimate was made, by whom, or what the value of those gold francs might be in today's currency. Perhaps a more understandable picture of the valuables stored in the treasury and used for decoration in the palaces is given by the historian Diodorus Siculus, who says that Alexander used thirty thousand camels and countless donkeys to carry off those treasures.

As the moon rose, silvering the ruined city, we agreed that we would have felt a little better if it had not been Alexander who was responsible for the destruction, for we found it hard to believe him guilty of so pointless an atrocity. If only it had been an earthquake, or a barbarian tribe swooping down! But soon we came to the obvious conclusion that if Alexander had not done it, someone else would have; and at least Alexander had the foresight to have the Persian libraries translated before he destroyed them. Further regrets at human folly seemed childish, so we perched in silence on the hill and watched the silent city glittering in the moonlight.

The following day we made our pilgrimage to the royal necropolis, Naksh-i-Rustam, some four miles to the north of Persepolis, to see the huge sculptured tombs, cut into bare rock, of four kings of kings. The only one that has been positively identified, from inscriptions over the entranceway and on friezes, is that of Darius I. The other identifications that have been suggested are Artaxerxes I, Xerxes, and Darius II.

In front of the tombs stands a small, rectangular tower known as the shrine of Zoroaster, although there is no reason to believe that that is in fact what it was. It almost certainly, however, served some religious purpose, and may well have been the center of a wide garden, where, among royal statues, priests sang sacred songs and chanted hymns in praise of the monarchs buried there. Trying to conjure up visions of those priests and their acolytes, we began to wonder why the Persepolis procession had confined itself almost exclusively to warriors, for the Persian dynasts, although they were frequently engaged in wars of offense, were also defenders of the state religion, great builders, and patrons of the arts and sciences. But perhaps for a country determined to reestablish its national identity, the armed services seemed the most suitable symbols.

The same themes are to be found in the Sassanian bas-reliefs carved in the rock beneath the tombs. The most famous of these depicts the defeated Roman emperor Valerian paying homage to Shapur I. Not surprisingly, this was a very popular subject with sculptors serving the Shapur kings, for it was one of the chief events of their reigns. Another depicts Ardashir, the founder of the dynasty, receiving the emblem of sovereignty from the god called Ahuramazda, while the king's horse tramples his enemies.

Fifty miles north of Persepolis, in a wide featureless plain, lie the more ancient ruins of Pasargadae, the capital of Cyrus the Great, the first Achaemenian dynast. It was never so impressive as Persepolis, and the elements have been more unkind to it. Its chief site is the simple, now empty tomb of Cyrus. Plutarch says that an inscription on the tomb read, "I am Cyrus, the king, the Achaemenian," while another ancient historian phrases it this way, "I, Cyrus, king of kings, lie here." Unfortunately, the inscription, however it read, vanished ages ago, as did the earthly remains of the mighty king whose 2500th anniversary celebrations brought so many fellow heads of state to Persepolis in the month of October, 1971.

18-23. The 2500th anniversary celebration held at the ruins of Persepolis (*preceding page*) was climaxed by a solemn procession representing the chief Iranian dynasties: *right*, Achaemenian; *below*, Arsacid; *opposite above*, Saffarid; *opposite below*, Sassanian; and *overleaf*, a march-past by corpsmen of the shah's white revolution.

24-25. Spectators at the procession (*below*) included fifty heads of state or their representatives. At the Aryamehr Stadium in Tehran (*opposite*) an ancient sports display was held to mark the celebrations.

26-29. Persepolis, founded by Darius in 520 B.C. was the Achaemenian capital until it was destroyed by Alexander the Great. The palace of Xerxes, his son, is seen on the preceding page, but according to historians it did not compare with the more elaborate interior from the palace of Darius shown on this page.

30-31. The Hall of One Hundred Columns in the palace of Darius was used for royal audiences. Each column is forty feet high; *below*, detail of a decorated relief; *opposite*, one of eight sculptured entranceways.

32-35. The Apadana, also known as the "kingliest palace," was begun by Darius and completed by Xerxes; *right*, detail showing the repeated lion-bull motif; *below*, a view of the famous stairway; *opposite*, the ruins of the main hall; and *overleaf*, the Apadana at sunset.

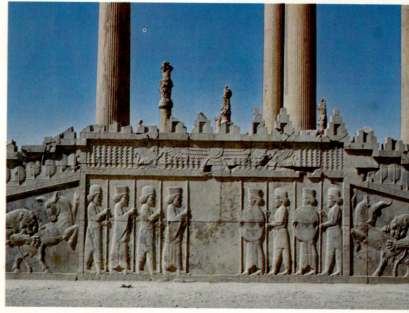

Oases and Other Places

From Shiraz we were to make our way to Tehran, the capital, but for this journey we spurned the easy national highway that heads directly north through Isfahan, taking instead what the map calls "a second-class (dust) road" westward to Kazerun, where we then drove in a northwesterly direction all the way to the Caspian Sea before turning toward Tehran. We knew that the road would be difficult at times, and perhaps even occasionally dangerous, but we were determined to see at least a part of Iran that lay off the beaten tourist track. Before we reached the Iranian shore of the Caspian, we traversed steep mountain gorges, patches of desert, oil fields, and towns that had not often received foreign visitors, let alone an exotic group of dusty (and often thirsty) camera laden Japanese.

Our first short patch of road zigzagged between the cliffs of the Zagros mountain range, and we were by no means averse to a stop at Kazerun, a pleasant little town of twenty-odd thousand situated on a plateau nearly three thousand feet above sea level. The plateau is famous for its tobacco as well as for rice and cotton. At a thriving little market in the town, I bought a pair of heavy cotton slippers lined with brilliantly colored leather. I found them the most comfortable ones I had ever owned, and after a long day of picture taking I used to take off my heavy leather boots and ease my tired feet into those soft, handsome slippers with a deep sigh of relief.

Of course I had to bargain for them. That was expected there, as elsewhere in this part of the world, and had I failed to do so I would not only have lost face but also grievously disappointed the seller. Bargaining in the Zagros Mountains is a particularly long and loud process, which begins with the seller quoting a price so obviously ridiculous and exorbitant that the prospective buyer can only reply with a profound wail of despair. He then, after a while, suggests a price so low that it produces a counter-wail from the merchant. This is the beginning, and if all goes well the haggling will eventually end, after quite a long time, in a compromise suitable to both parties. And both parties will have enjoyed the game.

These inhabitants of the Zagros Mountains are a people unto themselves, quite unlike the mountain-dwelling folk of northern Iran, who are jolly and outgoing and fond of whatever simple pleasures of life they can afford. Here in the Zagros range, the people seemed silent and thoughtful, with a sullen, frequently stormy expression. We wondered about the cause of this and finally decided that it lay in their long isolation from the rest of the world and the need to defend their terrain from the invader with their own arms and hands.

Another quality that struck us forcefully was their apparent good health. Remote from clever doctors and modern hospitals, they glow with ruddy well-being, their skin is lustrous and beautifully tinted, and their eyesight is as keen as that of an eagle. They have evolved a complex communal organization based apparently on mutual trust and, or so it seemed to us, a wariness of strangers.

After fortifying ourselves in Kazerun with some dried apricots, we headed southward along the twenty-mile road that leads through a deep gorge to the ancient capital of the three Sassanian kings who bore the name of Shapur. Here the dark yellow cliffs, largely limestone, sandstone, and granite, are steep and bare and forbidding, and as we drove toward the south we encountered only occasional nomads, some of them engaged in carpet weaving by the roadside.

Finally we descended to the Shapur River, which now in midsummer was barely a trickle, although a heavily draped woman in black was doing her best to wash the family laundry in the shallow, fishy, reedy water, while a great multitude of yellow butterflies flitted about her head. High over the cliffs above us, we saw eagles soaring in their search for prey. Here and there in the valley were the tents of nomads and the huts of farmers. Watching a shepherd huddled in the shadow of an overhanging cliff to avoid the hot, bright sunlight, I wondered where he would be sleeping that night. Probably, I decided (like us) under the starry sky.

Beyond the river lie the ruins of Bishapur, chiefly famous now for the rock carvings depicting the exploits of the Sassanian kings. Some of the scenes can no longer be interpreted; others tell the same stories as those in the necropolis at Persepolis, while just north of Kazerun there is yet another relief repeating the obeisance of the defeated Valerian before the victorious Shapur I.

Back on the road north, we soon entered a land of oil fields and deserts. One of the world's three chief exporters of oil, Iran nationalized the oil industry in 1951 to protect its natural resources, and now the National Iranian Oil Company is the biggest in the world. The port of Abadan, on the Persian Gulf, connected by pipelines to three large oil fields, has a refinery capable of producing some twenty million tons of petroleum annually. The most modern installations permit tankers to load up either right at the quay or standing offshore. It is interesting to realize that this same oil was used to fuel the ancient Zoroastrian fires and to caulk boats, as well as to provide such instruments of war as fire-tipped arrows and flaming cauldrons. Today, as yesterday, some of the oil inevitably finds its way into engines of destruction. Twenty-five centuries of progress?

What is progress, we asked as we drove along, but we did not stay for an answer, for the temperature seemed to soar almost to boiling point and the country was so arid as to suggest that it seldom saw a raindrop from one year to the next. From time to time we felt so dehydrated that we used some of our precious store of water to pour cupfuls over our heads. It was a land that seemed to defy humanity.

Then, as we rose onto a semidesert plateau, the temperature seemed to rise too, if that indeed was possible. There were no trees, virtually no vegetation, only great stretches of glaringly white land, strewn with huge, misshapen boulders, which gave the landscape an unearthly look, as though we had somehow wandered onto an alien planet. It would have been helpful, we decided, to be wearing air-cooled space suits.

The land is crisscrossed by deep gullies, through which melted ice flows in winter from the mountains beyond. As a result, there are torrents and floods, which cause landslides and dash great rocks from one place to another as though they were tiny pebbles. These torrents never reach the sea, however, for the surrounding land is so dry that it soaks up water like a sponge. There is a short while in spring when a few blades of grass shoot up, but they die very soon, and when we were there in midsummer, the world seemed dead and the gullies looked like blazing furnaces. It would have been certain death to venture out.

Strangely enough, man somehow contrives to live in this most inhospitable world, and he does so in tiny oases, which huddle around thin streams of water trickling up from underground.

There are seldom more, usually less, than one hundred inhabitants in these desert oases. It is obviously a hard life, very nearly an impossible one, and a remarkable tribute to man's insistence upon adapting himself to conditions that one might suppose were quite beyond his powers.

The struggle for survival in these Moslem villages must inevitably breed a hardened attitude toward life. One day we watched a group of women gathered around the communal well. As they waited to fill their jugs, one woman inadvertently knocked over the jug that another woman had placed on a nearby ledge, smashing it to pieces. The first woman uttered no word of apology, for apology would have meant acceptance of responsibility; she merely murmured laconically that it was the will of God that the jug be broken that day. (This attitude is, of course, widespread in Mohammedan countries: a beggar, for instance, if given alms, will not thank the giver but rather will thank Allah, for having inspired the giver to bestow alms.)

In this particular case, the woman whose jug was broken refused to agree that the catastrophe was God's fault. She hurled herself upon the other, and there ensued a vicious fight, the two women pummeling, kicking, and scratching one another. The woman who had broken the jug emerged victorious, thus proving that she was right in putting the blame upon God. The defeated woman now presumably had no choice but to agree. Had she not, the husbands might have felt bound to enter the altercation, and perhaps a blood feud might have resulted, lasting for their lifetime.

Food, of course, is extremely scarce in these villages, for water is insufficient to grow an adequate amount of grain, and there is precious little pasture to feed the few sheep that provide the only source of meat for these oasis dwellers. Although pigs are easier to breed and nourish in these conditions, their flesh is taboo for orthodox Moslems who still follow the teachings of the Koran.

As might be expected, people who lead such harsh lives do not at first take kindly to strangers, but we were surprised and pleased to discover that once we had entered the village teahouse, we were welcomed with warm smiles. Every community, no matter how small or poor, has at least one such teahouse, which serves as a meeting place for the men (not the women, of course) of the village. There, under the soothing influence of the scent and sweetness of the tea, tongues are loosened to the point of loquacity, and the usually taciturn desert dwellers exchange bits of information and gossip and even begin to engage in competitive boastfulness. The teahouse offers one of the few means of escaping, even briefly, from the harsh tedium of desert life.

As we continued northward, the white rocky cliffs gradually darkened and then turned a brilliant red as the sinking sun set the whole world ablaze. We entered the prosperous town of Kermanshah, lying in a cool, fertile plateau some five thousand feet above sea level. Its population of over two hundred thousand consists mainly of Kurds.

Founded at the end of the fourth century A.D. by Bahram IV, a monarch of the Sassanian dynasty, who had earlier been governor of Kerman Province (and thus named the city after himself, the Kerman shah), it has had a stormy, typically Iranian history of occupation, destruction, and liberation. As a result, although the town itself now boasts a large oil refinery, it has no ancient monuments of importance, except for two superb sights nearby: Taq-i-Bustan and Bistam.

The nearer of the two, Taq-i-Bustan lies only a few miles to the east and consists of two caves decorated inside and out with handsome Sassanian bas-reliefs. Depicted there are events, real or legendary, from the lives of three of Bahram's predecessors on the Sassanian throne and one of his late successors. The ones of

Chosroes II Parvez, his successor, found in the second cave are the most striking, for the reliefs, though obviously idealized, show us what were no doubt actual events: the monarch embarked on two hunts, one for wild boar and one for stags.

At Bistam, twenty-odd miles from Kermanshah, Darius I fought and won a decisive battle, and in commemoration he had a relief carved two hundred feet above the ground on a rock face overlooking the ancient Silk Road. The relief depicts Darius's success in putting down a revolt of tributary satraps led by a disloyal younger son of Cyrus. A chiseled inscription in three languages—Old Persian, Neo-Babylonian, and Neo-Elamite—has proved of invaluable assistance to scholars of ancient Mesopotamian civilization.

From Kermanshah we headed in a northeasterly direction, through rich fields of wheat and barley, toward the town of Hamadan, stopping on the way at Lahijan, a small village, where in olden days some of Iran's most beautiful pottery was produced. Although today the production is limited to articles of daily use, ordinary water jugs and jars, the village is still famous throughout the country for its pottery, and piled high on both sides of its narrow lanes were brightly colored pieces that, although they may no longer be sought after by connoisseurs, made a brave and happy show.

It was a pleasant little village, and we spent several drowsy days there, watching the potters at work as they mixed their colors and glazes, shaped their jars, and fired them in underground kilns, just like those of ancient times. The rays of the sun, filtering into the workshops through small holes in the ceiling, made fascinating patterns. Then, in late afternoon, we would wander along fields of amber wheat, yellow dandelions, and red poppies and watch the setting sun turn the mud walls of the houses from pale pink to deep purple.

Hamadan is also an extremely ancient city. Like Persepolis, it is attributed to the mythical Jamshid, and like Kermanshah, it has known an endless procession of invaders, including Alexander, Timur, and the armies of the Ottoman sultans. But unlike Kermanshah, it has managed to retain a few of its ancient monuments; one of the most interesting is a stone lion that was largely destroyed by invading Dailamites but is still thought by the people of Hamadan to possess magical properties, like the ability to provide food and clothing to the needy.

For many centuries Hamadan was also a place of Jewish pilgrimage. Legend has it that Queen Esther, the consort of King Ahasuerus (now identified by scholars as Xerxes), and her cousin Mordecai are buried here. In the Bible, Esther and Mordecai succeeded in thwarting the Grand Vizier Haman's desire to exterminate the Jews in the Persian Empire; and once having accomplished his downfall, Mordecai became grand vizier in his place. The ancient Hebrew spring festival of Purim is said to celebrate this delivery, and pious Jews came to Hamadan to pay their respects to the deliverers. Alas for legend, recent scholarly investigation has shown that the little mausoleum still to be seen in Hamadan never contained the body of Queen Esther but most probably that of another Jewish consort, Queen Shushan Dokht, who was taken in marriage by the Sassanian king, Yazdegerd I (A.D. 339–420).

Hamadan's other claim to fame is that the great Islamic philosopher known to the world as Avicenna spent the last years of his life there, died there, and was buried there. A fine modern mausoleum has been erected to his memory. The poet Baba Taher, who lived in Hamadan around the same time, in the first half of the eleventh century, lies buried nearby.

An important trading and communications center, Hamadan, situated at an altitude of over six thousand feet, is a much frequented summer resort. Its winters, however, are notoriously long and very, very cold, with heavy snowfalls caused by nearby Mount Alvand, which rises to a height of nearly twelve thousand feet.

Our next stop lay at the end of a long drive north, through mountain passes, across high plateaus, and beside the sloping green hills of Zenjan. In the course of our journey we attracted a number of four-footed friends as well as potential enemies. Rabbits, foxes, and unfamiliar beasts resembling polecats dashed across the road as we approached, barking sheep dogs raced us from time to time, and at night we heard unearthly howls that could have come from either wolves or, we hoped, dogs.

Once we had crossed the steep pass of the northerly Elburz range of mountains, we began our descent into the Gilan Province; it and neighboring Mazandaran, make up the fertile green territory that borders the Caspian Sea. Characterized by a heavy annual rainfall and a subtropical climate, this is in a very real sense the breadbasket of a country that possesses such a small proportion of arable land. Crops include rice, cotton, and tea.

Fortunately for us, our car did not break down until we were out of the mountains, but not until about four in the morning did we manage to get it going again. As a result, we scurried through the town of Rasht, reserving our visit there for another day, for we were by then eager to reach our destination, the Caspian port of Bandar-e Pahlavi. The sun had already risen by the time we saw the sea, and the temperature, even at that early hour, seemed as hot as a midsummer noon in Tokyo.

The Caspian Sea, with a total area of nearly one hundred and fifty thousand square miles, is bordered only on the south by Iran, on its other sides by the Soviet Union. It is the largest land-locked body of water in the world, and the breeding ground of three varieties of sturgeon, from which Iran's famous caviar is produced. The first organized attempt to process caviar was made here at Bandar-e Pahlavi in 1896 by a Russian family, who had been granted an Iranian government fishing concession. Not until 1953 did a wholly state-owned corporation take over, which now has its headquarters there, with a well-known research institute and a prosperous processing plant. It is not Iranians alone who claim that their caviar is the best in the world, and it has the further advantage, we discovered, of being quite reasonably priced—at least by international standards.

In some ways this littoral district of Iran, with its tea and rice fields, reminded us of our native Japan, but when we tried to take pictures of women bending over the plants, we received no politely phrased invitations, as we would have at home. Instead, we were shouted at, and children hurled balls of mud at us. We found that experience, plus the heat, rather discouraging, and were not sorry to continue on eastward into the shade of the thick forests of Mazandaran.

We stopped at a couple of beach resorts, Ramsar and Babol Sar, both very pleasant and restful. The comfortable hotels and the handsome beaches made quite an astonishing change from the desert waste lands and the high mountains we had passed through to get here. So too did the scenery: instead of heavily draped women, for all intents and purposes invisible, there were attractive young girls wearing bikinis as scanty as any seen on the French Riviera.

Our pleasure at the sight, however, was not shared by everyone. As we lay on the beach admiring the view, along came an elderly, robed gentleman, whom we took to be an *imam*, or Mohammedan priest. Pointing scornfully at the bikini clad girls, he cried, "Shame! Shame!" Just then a young woman waded out of the water wearing a swimming costume as voluminous as an old-fashioned nightgown. She approached the elderly and still indignant gentleman, whom she addressed submissively as her father.

Later, we told a young Iranian with whom we had become acquainted about the incident. He laughed and shrugged, re-marking, "Well, if the times don't suit you, then you've got to suit yourself to the times." We were not quite certain how to interpret this rather cryptic remark but decided not to pursue the matter any further, at least for the moment.

We had only one more stop to make before Tehran, and that was the town of Sari, which has a reputation in Iran for two things: its deer park and its *baghali polo*. On Fridays, the Moslem sabbath, families come out from Tehran to Sari to picnic on *baghali polo*. Since it appeared to be only a dish of rice mixed with beans and raisins, we were not unduly impressed and thought it compared rather poorly with some of the truly exquisite exam-ples of Iranian *haute cuisine*. In fact, we decided not to dawdle any longer but to continue right on to Tehran, which, along with its other amenities, offers the visitor a wide choice among a number of fine restaurants—and all the caviar and vodka he wants, or can afford.

36. Shapur was the name of three Sassanian monarchs and also of the Sassanian capital. Today, in the Bishapur Valley, a farmer ploughs his land with oxen (*preceding page*).

37-38. The remains of the Shapur rock carvings show the triumph of Bahram II (*below*), the investiture of Bahram I and the triumph of Shapur II (*opposite*).

39-42. Lahijan, a village close to Rasht, famous in ancient times for its beautiful ceramics, is still a pottery center. The village craftsmen use the old kilns, which are situated underground below the workshops. *Opposite*, the pots are left to dry in the sun after they are fired in the kiln.

43. One of the country's fertile areas is the rich pastureland in the mountains near Zenjan (*overleaf*) where sheep are raised.

44-47. *Below*, the triumph of Darius at Bistam near Kermanshah; *right* and *opposite left*, two scenes showing a boar hunt; *opposite right*, detail of the acanthus leaf motif at Taq-i-Bustan.

48-49. Although barley and wheat are the main cereal crops of Iran, rice is also grown in the Caspian Sea provinces. Here women in brilliant costume work in the paddies at Rasht.

50. Fishing is an important industry at Bandar-e Pahlavi (*right*).

51-55. Caviar is a recent export. When the tiny sturgeons (*below left*) are four inches long they are released into the Caspian Sea. The caviar research institute (*below right*) is located at Bandar-e Pahlavi. The beach along the Caspian Sea seen at sunset is an ideal spot for children to amuse themselves (*opposite* and *overleaf*).

Tapestry of the Future

The capital, naturally enough, is where the visitor becomes most keenly aware of the "new Iran," the Iran of the shahanshah's white revolution. Now a bustling city of three million, which only a few years ago was little more than a large town, Tehran continues to expand, energetically putting up huge new factories and bright modern housing projects for the workers; comfortable tourist hotels (including of course a branch of the ubiquitous Hilton); broad new avenues crowded with private cars, double-deck buses, and glowing orange taxis; new hospitals, schools and colleges, whose paths are lined with rose bushes; government buildings—the list, in fact, is very nearly endless, for under royal impetus Tehran is transforming itself with unbelievable rapidity into a great contemporary metropolis.

Compared with other Iranian capitals of former days, it is not by any means an old city, a fact which has been extremely useful to the present-day government in its modernization program, for there have been virtually no ancient and hallowed impediments to expansion. Although there was apparently a settled community on the site as early as the ninth century A.D., it remained a small provincial town until 1785, when Agha Mohammed Khan, founder of the Qajar dynasty, made it his capital. Although it has remained the national capital, its growth was modest until the election of the present monarch's father in 1925. Since then, both its population and area have doubled and perhaps even quadrupled.

It has been a most astonishing phenomenon, comparable in some ways to the extraordinary growth of my own capital after its destruction during the Second World War. Much of the credit for this must go to the monarch and his white revolution, which was designed to bring the nation from its ancient feudal past into the modern world. Begun in 1963, the white revolution is based ultimately on twelve points, one of the most important of which was the redistribution of land and the abolition of the peasant-landlord tenure system.

Other points included government sponsored incentives to increase private production; the formation of a literacy corps to combat "illiteracy, superstition, and ignorance"; the establishment of a health corps to improve sanitary conditions and to provide free medical treatment to deprived rural areas; the total reorganization of both the government and the national educational system; the nationalization of the country's water resources in order to equalize the distribution of fresh water; the establishment of local courts in small villages to provide justice to all citizens; and lastly "the amendment of the electoral system to grant voting and other related rights to women," including the right to hold national office.

It is an ambitious program indeed, and one that seems to be working well although a single decade is too brief a time to accomplish so many reforms without a revolutionary change of government. "We had great industrial potential," the shahanshah himself wrote in 1963, "that could be vastly developed." These are not mere words: from what I could see His Majesty's expectations have met with the whole-hearted approval of the Iranians.

Half of them, it should be borne in mind, are the newly enfranchised women of Iran, for whom the royal edict of 1963 was revolutionary indeed. The role of the female in Islamic society has not always been a happy one. Not only has she been traditionally the slave of her master in this world but she has also been barred from the heaven that her husband could look forward to upon his death. She was usually veiled, frequently confined within the walls of her father's, then her husband's, house, and in some countries was one of many wives. Her husband could dispose of her merely by repeating "I divorce you" three times, although she herself did not possess the same right, and she might be stoned to death for adultery.

In Iran today women have been elected to parliament, have entered the judiciary, and have advanced to high positions in the government. Divorces are no longer automatic but are referred to special courts for settlement, and girls are no longer sold by their fathers to a husband they may never have seen before marriage. This, at any rate, is true in the cities; in the more backward rural areas, social custom has probably changed less than expected. There, I was told, polygamy still exists, the role of the woman remains subservient, and the men still prefer new mosques to new schools.

When I questioned an Iranian friend, a young engineer who studied in Japan, about the future of his country under the white revolution, he was highly optimistic, but at the same time he blamed the state religion for Iran's backwardness compared to other countries that have moved out of the nineteenth century and into the twentieth. "During periods of social ferment," he said, "religion becomes the bulwark of reaction. And the stronger the bond between state and church, the more quickly people flee to the haven of religion, preferring the assurance it offers to the uncertainty that material progress entails."

After a moment's thought, he went on: "Once upon a time

my country flourished under Islam, but more recently Iran has been brought by Islam to the brink of disaster. Now, however, with the white revolution transforming the nation, we will soon be as green and prosperous as we deserve to be, with our rich natural resources, the native energy of our people, and—never forget it!—our long history of civilization."

One very hopeful signpost to the future of Iran is the emancipation of women. I have seen young girls and women working in factories, laboratories, offices, and government bureaus, some holding positions of considerable importance. When I asked whether there was hostility toward these women from men in inferior posts, I was told that probably there was less ill feeling here in Iran than in some Western countries, where women are still waging an all-out war for "liberation."

Here they have not, of course, achieved the absolute equality that some of their Western sisters seek, but when one sees thousands of happy and healthy girls rehearsing for the Asian Games (to be held in Tehran in 1974), one cannot help comparing them with their oppressed counterparts in the feudal sheikdoms— veiled and shrouded prisoners who cannot call their minds or souls, let alone their bodies, their own. Then one realizes that Iran has come a very long way in a very short time, and there seems to be no reason why it should not continue to advance along the path it has chosen for itself.

Of course there is a great deal to see and do in the spirited new capital aside from admiring the evidence of its recent social and economic progress. Its museums are one attraction. Although it boasts no great ancient monuments, those museums are an unbelievably rich storehouse of treasures dating all the way back to prehistoric days. Of prime importance, of course, is the splendidly arranged archaeological museum, the Iran Bastan, which contains objects dating as far back as the fifth millennium B.C. Among its more famous possessions are gold and silver treasures from various archaeological sites around the country, including Persepolis. These are all displayed on the ground floor, while the floor above is devoted to Islamic art: ceramics, illuminated manuscripts, brocades and carpets, intricately decorated *mihrab* (niches) and *minbar* (pulpits) from old mosques, and lovely carved alabaster windows. A few hours, or even better, a few days, spent in the Iran Bastan is living proof that Persians have for thousands of years been superb artists and craftsmen.

Then there is the Golestan (or Rose Garden) Palace, built over a hundred years ago in a most enchanting garden, with blue-tiled pools beneath wide spreading shade trees. Here, displayed in a grand hall, are priceless objects of art, including rugs and enameled works, gifts from foreign monarchs, and royal regalia, including the famous Peacock Throne, set upon a dais at the end of the hall. On state occasions the shahanshah gives audience and receives distinguished foreign visitors, and it was here that the coronation ceremonies for both Shah Aryamehr and Empress Farah were held.

The fabulous crown jewels of Iran may be admired within the sanctuary of the Markazi Bank, where they are kept. Aside from the two imperial crowns and lesser coronets, there is a bewildering profusion of mounted and unmounted gems, of ropes of pearls (some as large as pigeons' eggs), of gem encrusted swords, and of other rare, beautiful, and valuable objects. The most famous of the diamonds is the Sea of Light, and the most famous of the stones and one that is said to be unique in the world is a flawless emerald three inches long and two inches wide set on top of a snuff box. The overall value of the jewels is discreetly unmentioned, but the fact that they serve as the backing for the currency of oil-rich Iran may give an indication of their value.

By comparison, the smaller museums of Tehran are a bit of an anticlimax, but nevertheless well worth a visit. The most note-worthy are the Museum of Decorative Arts, the National Art Museum, devoted to displays of contemporary Iranian arts and crafts, and the Ethnological Museum, which houses a remarkable collection of modern reproductions of ancient Iranian costumes draped on wax figures.

Tehran has two major nineteenth-century mosques: the Masjid-i-Sepahsalar, containing an important Islamic library including five thousand manuscripts, and the Masjid-i-Shah, the Royal Mosque, put up during the reign of Fath Ali Shah, a Qajar monarch. Of considerable interest also is the Marble Palace, built by Reza Shah and formerly used as a residence by the royal family. It was recently donated to the nation by the monarch to serve as a Pahlavi dynasty museum.

Rudaki Hall offers a regular series of concerts, operas, and ballets, as well as performances of Iranian dances. For sports en-thusiasts, one of the most fascinating places in Tehran is the Zurkaneh (The House of Strength), where ancient Iranian gym-nastics, exhibited at royal courts in the past, are still practiced to a traditional musical accompaniment. There are also, of course, the more familiar spectator sports: soccer and basketball, boxing and wrestling, even polo, which some historians believe was first played in Iran during the reign of Darius the Great.

Speaking of spectator sports, I must not omit one which, although it may not be considered a true sport, certainly attracts spectators—the famous Islamic art of belly dancing. At nightclubs that specialize in this exotic form of entertainment, the dancers gyrate their bodies to an ever-increasing tempo until the top half almost seems to fly away from the lower half. As the staccato beat of the drums grows faster and the desertlike wail of the music more piercing, dancers and spectators both become more excited. After the dance is over, the girls will accept invitations to a drink with alacrity. I had no doubt that their furious gyrations could induce quite a thirst.

Another popular activity in Tehran is shopping, which for the tourist means hunting for souvenirs to take home with him. He may choose to shop in the modern stores on broad, tree lined streets, but he will find Tehran's covered bazaar more exciting. It is the largest in the country, and also thought to be the largest in the Middle East. As in all such bazaars in the Islamic world, there is a bewildering maze of narrow lanes filled with a constant throng of buyers and would-be buyers, looking at the wares in tiny stalls. Here, as elsewhere, sellers of similar goods tend to congregate in one area; and here, as elsewhere, bargaining is essential, since no one, not even a gullible tourist, is expected to pay the first price asked. The result is a soulful clamor that adds to the happy confusion beneath its roofs.

On Friday, Tehran pretty much shuts down, and its people go off into the country on picnics and excursions or, in winter, into the nearby mountains to ski. Or they may, as we did, investigate some of the ancient sites in the vicinity. Rey, for example, although it has little to offer the tourist today, is of paramount interest to the historian and archaeologist, since it is one of the oldest continuously inhabited sites in the world. Only five miles southeast of the capital, it is the center of extensive ruins, which have been excavated by an American expedition. Artifacts dating back to the fifth millenium B.C. have been found in the ruins, which means that people have been living in Rey for seven or eight thousand years or longer.

Shards of painted pottery of similar date (now in the Iran Bastan) have also been found in a neighboring mound called the Tepe Chesmeh Ali. One day we made our own archaeological investigation at the village of Saveh, about one hundred miles southwest of Tehran. When we arrived, we found that the people of the village were digging up an old road beneath a damaged minaret. As they dug, they turned up innumerable potsherds, beautifully colored, which they tossed aside like so many bits of junk.

Seeing our interest, a little boy told us there were some ancient mounds nearby and offered to lead us to them. This sort of mound is known in Arabic as a *tall* or *tell* and in Iranian as a *tepe*. One of the mounds seemed to be virtually untouched, and we wondered excitedly if we would come across anything of interest. As we stood there talking, a tall, slender, middle-aged gentleman of olive skin and noble mien appeared suddenly out of nowhere and offered his help.

This we gladly accepted and watched with growing excitement as he came up with broken bits of pottery, some of pure deep Persian blue, some with patterns of light blue and black, some with lines drawn in deep blue on a white ground. After a time, it began to grow dark and the digging had to stop, so we paid the kind and helpful gentleman his modest fee and then sat atop the ancient hillock, watching the great, golden sun sink into the distant desert. As we sat and waited, the moon rose, a disk that seemed as large and fiery-colored as the sun that had just disappeared. When the moon rose higher, the red drained out of it, and the world about us, the hillock, the little village, the distant desert, turned to pale silver.

Gold and silver: the colors of the great treasures of ancient Persia. We knew that the memory of that desert sunset and moonrise would be with us for a long time, and we felt highly pleased, as we returned to Tehran with our treasures, a few bits of old blue pottery, that once we too had walked in one of the world's most ancient civilizations.

56-60. Tehran: the snowcapped Elburz Mountains in the distance (*preceding page*); Boulevard Elizabeth II (*right*); stained glass is used to decorate the doors of homes (*below*); Rudaki Hall (*opposite*) has performances of ballet, opera, concerts and Iranian dances.

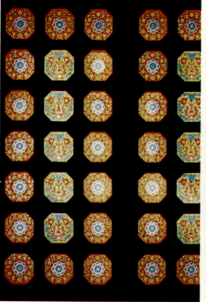

61-63. The many faces and places of Tehran: *right*, a young girl in a traditional shawl; *below*, girls visit a community washing place in the covered bazaar; *opposite*, large loaves of bread are sold in the markets.

64–66. The wedding ceremony (*right* and *below*) of an affluent young couple took place in a huge colored tent and was attended by over five hundred guests.

67–68. *Zurkaneh* (*opposite*) is an ancient form of wrestling performed to the accompaniment of music. Roses are always thrown at the spectators.

69-71. The shah's fifty-second birthday celebration (*below*) was held at Golestan Palace; its magnificent interior (*right* and *opposite*) includes the grand hall, where ancient works of art, carpets and enameled work are displayed.

72-77. Ancient gold and silver treasures are housed in the Iran Bastan (Tehran's archaeological museum): *right*, a cup from Marlik; *below*, metalwork from Ziwiyeh; *opposite above*, the tablet of Darius II from Hamadan and a decorated plate from Ziwiyeh; *opposite below*, two vases from Gilan.

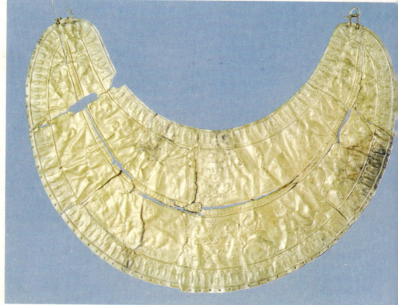

78-81. Fabrics displayed in the Museum of Decorative Arts: *below*, nineteenth-century chain-stitched woolen cloth from Kerman; *right*, brocade with gold thread, also nineteenth century; *opposite left*, velvet embroidered in silk and gold, from the eighteenth century; and *opposite right*, a sixteenth-century piece of silk brocade with gold thread (from the Iran Bastan).

82-85. Persian vases in the Iran Bastan: *right*, from Saveh (thirteenth century); *below left*, from Gorgan (thirteenth century); *below right*, from Mesopotamia (ninth or tenth century); *opposite*, from Persepolis (ninth century).

86. This priceless crown studded with 26,733 precious
stones was made for the coronation of Fath Ali Shah
in 1798.

THIS BEAUTIFUL WORLD